P9-CNA-805

MISSISSIPPI

by Jonatha A. Brown
and Frances E. Ruffin

GARETH**STEVENS**
PUBLISHING
A Member of the WRC Media Family of Companies

Please visit our web site at: www.garethstevens.com
For a free color catalog describing Gareth Stevens Publishing's
list of high-quality books and multimedia programs, call
1-800-542-2595 (USA) or 1-800-387-3178 (Canada).
Gareth Stevens Publishing's fax: (877) 542-2596.

Library of Congress Cataloging-in-Publication Data

Brown, Jonatha A.
    Mississippi / Jonatha A. Brown and Frances E. Ruffin.
       p. cm. — (Portraits of the states)
    Includes bibliographical references and index.
    ISBN-10: 0-8368-4670-2   ISBN-13: 978-0-8368-4670-6 (lib. bdg.)
    ISBN-10: 0-8368-4689-3   ISBN-13: 978-0-8368-4689-8 (softcover)
    1. Mississippi—Juvenile literature.   I. Ruffin, Frances E.
    II. Title.   III. Series.
    F341.3.B76   2006
    976.2—dc22   2005054184

Updated edition reprinted in 2007. First published in 2006 by
Gareth Stevens Publishing
A Weekly Reader Company
1 Reader's Digest Rd.
Pleasantville, NY 10570-7000 USA

Copyright © 2006 by Gareth Stevens, Inc.

Editorial direction: Mark J. Sachner
Project manager: Jonatha A. Brown
Editor: Catherine Gardner
Art direction and design: Tammy West
Picture research: Diane Laska-Swanke
Indexer: Walter Kronenberg
Production: Jessica Morris and Robert Kraus

Picture credits: Cover, pp. 4, 16, courtesy of the Mississippi Development
Authority/Division of Tourism; p. 5 © ArtToday; p. 6 © MPI/Getty Images;
p. 8 © Three Lions/Getty Images; p. 9 © Stock Montage/Getty Images; p. 10
© Hulton Archive/Getty Images; p. 12 Mark Wolfe/FEMA; pp. 15, 20, 24, 25,
26, 27 © John Elk III; pp. 18, 22 © Philip Gould; p. 28 © Don Cravens/Time
& Life Pictures/Getty Images; p. 29 © Eliot J. Schechter/Getty Images

All rights reserved. No part of this book may be reproduced, stored in a retrieval
system, or transmitted in any form or by any means, electronic, mechanical,
photocopying, recording, or otherwise, without the prior written permission
of the copyright holder.

Printed in the United States of America

2 3 4 5 6 7 8 9 10 09 08 07

CONTENTS

★ ★

Words that are defined in the Glossary appear
in **bold** the first time they are used in the text.

On the Cover: A bridge spans the mighty Mississippi River at one of its
widest points.

Introduction

If you could visit Mississippi, where would you go? Would you head for the Mississippi River? This huge river gave the state its name, and it rolls right down the western border.

Perhaps you would like to visit Native American museums or Civil War battlefields. Mississippi is full of historic places. The people of this state are proud of their history, and they like to share it.

If you enjoy the outdoors, take a hike or a tour through a swamp. You might spot deer, turtles, and long-legged water birds. Who knows? You might even see a few alligators!

No matter where you go, you will have fun in this state. Welcome to Mississippi!

Rowan Oak is a lovely old house in Oxford. It was built before the Civil War.

The state flag of Mississippi.

MISSISSIPPI FACTS

- Became the 20th U.S. State: December 10, 1817
- Population (2006): 2,910,540
- Capital: Jackson
- Biggest Cities: Jackson, Gulfport, Biloxi, Hattiesburg
- Size: 46,907 square miles (121,489 square kilometers)
- Nickname: The Magnolia State
- State Tree: Magnolia
- State Flower: Magnolia
- State Land Mammal: White-tailed deer
- State Bird: Mockingbird

History

Native Americans were the first people to live in Mississippi. They arrived there thousands of years ago. By the 1500s, three tribes held most of the land. They were the Natchez, the Choctaw, and the Chickasaw.

The Spanish arrived in the 1500s. They had heard the land was rich in gold. In 1539, Hernando de Soto set out to find this gold. The next year, he and his men reached Mississippi. De Soto did not find gold, so he left.

Claiming the Land

In 1673, the French came. Jacques Marquette and Louis Jolliet led the way. They reached the area by traveling down the Mississippi River. Nine years later, Robert de La Salle claimed all of the land drained by the great river for France.

Jacques Marquette traveled hundreds of miles down the Mississippi River.

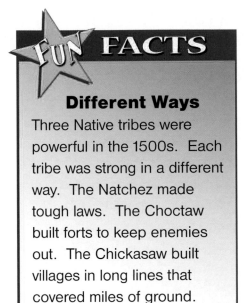

FUN FACTS

Different Ways

Three Native tribes were powerful in the 1500s. Each tribe was strong in a different way. The Natchez made tough laws. The Choctaw built forts to keep enemies out. The Chickasaw built villages in long lines that covered miles of ground.

The French took some of the Natchez's land. They built forts near where Ocean Springs and Natchez stand now. Settlers moved to the new **colony**. They grew cotton, rice, and other crops. Many brought African American slaves to work in the fields.

Fighting over the Land

The Natchez wanted their land back. The British wanted the land, too. Many Natives joined with Britain. They attacked the French in 1729. They fought for many years. In 1763, the British won. They took the land in Mississippi.

The British also held colonies on the Atlantic coast. These colonies soon wanted to be free of Britain. In 1775, they began to fight the Revolutionary War.

The colonies won the war in 1783. They formed the United States. They won all of the British lands east of

IN MISSISSIPPI'S HISTORY

The Spanish Return

During the Revolutionary War, Spain saw a chance to get some good land. It took over Natchez and the land along the Gulf of Mexico. In 1798, Spain gave up some of this land to the United States. Over the next few years, it gave up the rest of the land.

the Mississippi River. Now, most of Mississippi was held by the United States.

In 1798, Mississippi became a U.S. **territory**. Over the next few years, more land was added to the territory. It was split into two parts in 1817. One part became Alabama. The other became the state of Mississippi.

Thousands of settlers from the East moved to the

IN MISSISSIPPI'S HISTORY

King Cotton

Cotton grew well in the rich black soil of Mississippi. By 1860, more cotton was grown here than in any other U.S. state. People often said that cotton was "king" because it was the top crop in the state. It made Mississippi one of the wealthiest states in the nation.

state. Many raised cotton. Some built huge farms called **plantations**. Slaves planted and harvested the crops.

In the early 1800s, many Native Americans still lived in the state. The whites wanted them to leave. The state leaders convinced the Natives to give up their land. In the early 1830s, most of the Natives moved west.

This picture of cotton pickers was taken in 1938. The workers were not much better off than slaves.

Native Name

The name Mississippi comes from the words *mici zibi*. They are Native American words. They mean "great river" or "gathering in of all the waters."

Breaking Away

Slavery was common in most Southern states. It was rare in the North. Most people in the North thought slavery should be banned. The two sides could not agree. In 1860, the Southern states began to break away from the nation. Mississippi was the second state to **secede** from the **Union**.

Mississippi and other Southern states formed a new country. They named it the Confederate States of America.

Civil War

The North wanted the South to stay in the Union. They

In 1863, the North won the Battle of Vicksburg and took control of the Mississippi River.

began to fight in the Civil War in 1861.

Two years into the war, a big battle took place at Vicksburg. The Union Army blasted the city for six weeks. It also blocked the Mississippi River so supplies could not get through. In the end, the Southerners ran out of food and water. They had to give up.

In 1865, the North won the war. The U.S. Army ruled Mississippi for the next few years. In 1870, it became a U.S. state again.

After the War

After the war, slaves were set free. Even so, white people in the South did not treat them as equals. Mississippi passed

IN MISSISSIPPI'S HISTORY

Living in Caves

During the battle of Vicksburg, people dug caves in the town's steep hillsides. The caves kept them safe from bombs. Some caves had several rooms with rugs and furniture. The cave dwellers were safe from bombs, but they had to deal with snakes that lived in the caves!

In World War I and II, African American soldiers were kept apart from white soldiers.

Famous People of Mississippi

Medgar Evers

Born: July 2, 1925, near Decatur, Mississippi

Died: June 12, 1963, Jackson, Mississippi

Medgar Evers was an African American who grew up with segregation. He wanted to change the laws so all people would have the same rights. To do this, he joined a group called the National Association for the Advancement of Colored People (NAACP). He worked hard for equal rights. Some whites hated him for trying to change the laws. In 1963, a white man shot and killed him. Evers's death made him a hero to people who cared about equal rights.

unfair laws. The laws kept African Americans from voting. The laws also kept blacks and whites apart in public places. Mississippi was a **segregated** state, and black people had a very hard time there.

At this time, much of the state was in ruins. The price of cotton fell. Some farmers went broke. By the early 1900s, Mississippi was a very poor state. The African Americans who lived there were especially poor. Some left the state to find work in the North and the West.

The United States entered World War II in 1941. Men and women from Mississippi joined the fight. Military bases were built in the state, too. Farmers and **factories** produced food and supplies for the soldiers. These jobs

In 2005, Hurricane Katrina caused terrible damage in Biloxi and other cities on the Gulf Coast.

helped people in the state get back to work.

Fighting for Rights

In the mid-1950s, African Americans began to stand up for their rights. Tensions between whites and blacks grew. The U.S. Supreme Court ordered the University of Mississippi to accept black students in 1962. The school refused and a **riot** broke out. President John F. Kennedy sent soldiers to the school. They forced it to accept its first black student. The soldiers stayed for more than a year to keep order at the school.

By the late 1960s, the laws had been changed. African Americans now have the same rights as whites.

Hurricane Katrina

Hurricane Katrina slammed into Mississippi on August 29, 2005. It hit Louisiana and Alabama, too. Many people in the region were killed. During the storm, Biloxi and Gulfport were smashed by wind, rain, and flooding. Homes, schools, and businesses were ruined. The final costs will be huge. Rebuilding will take years. Katrina was one of the worst storms in U.S. history.

★ ★ ★ Time Line ★ ★ ★

8000 B.C.	The first Native people reach Mississippi.
1540	Hernando de Soto comes to Mississippi.
1682	Robert de La Salle claims the land drained by the Mississippi River for France.
1763	The British defeat the French and claim the land east of the Mississippi River.
1783	The United States gains the Mississippi area.
1817	Mississippi becomes the twentieth U.S. state.
Early 1830s	Most Native Americans leave Mississippi and move west.
1861	Mississippi leaves the Union. The Civil War begins.
1865	The Civil War ends. Mississippi begins passing laws that take away the rights of African Americans.
1870	Mississippi rejoins the Union.
1941–1945	The United States fights in World War II. The war brings jobs to Mississippi.
1962	President John F. Kennedy sends U.S. soldiers to the University of Mississippi so a black student can enroll there.
2005	Hurricane Katrina slams into Mississippi's Gulf Coast.

People

Almost three million people live in Mississippi. In most other states, more people live in cities and large towns than in the country. But Mississippi is different. In this state, more than five out of ten people live on farms and in small settlements in the country.

Just less than one-half of the people live in cities and towns. The largest city is Jackson. Gulfport and Biloxi are the next largest. Both of these cities were badly damaged by Hurricane Katrina in 2005.

Hispanics: In the 2000 U.S. Census, 1.4 percent of the people living in Mississippi called themselves Latino or Hispanic. Most of them or their relatives came from places where Spanish is spoken. They may come from different racial backgrounds.

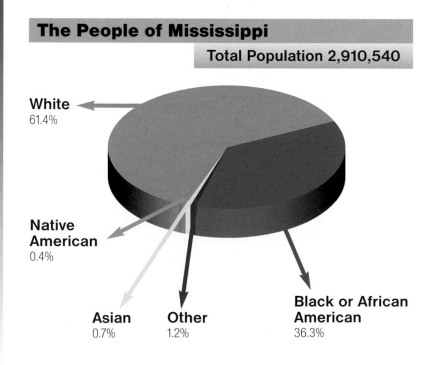

The People of Mississippi

Total Population 2,910,540

White
61.4%

Native American
0.4%

Asian
0.7%

Other
1.2%

Black or African American
36.3%

Percentages are based on the 2000 Census.

The People, Then and Now

Native Americans once had this land to themselves. Today, few Natives live in the state. Most of them are Choctaw. They live on a **reservation** in the east-central part of the state.

The first white settlers in the area were French. Large numbers of British settlers came next. People also moved here from the U.S. states along the East Coast. Many brought African

Jackson is the largest city in Mississippi. It is also the capital city. The dome of the state capitol is shown near the middle of this picture.

American slaves with them. The number of slaves grew quickly. For many years, African Americans made up the largest group in the state.

During and after World War II, many African Americans left Mississippi. They moved north and west,

The University of Southern Mississippi is in Hattiesburg. It was founded in 1910 and is now the second largest university in the state.

Education and Religion

The first free public school opened in 1821. It was in Columbus. Before 1910, some rural areas had no schools at all.

For many years, African Americans could not attend school. The first public school for black children opened in 1862. For the next century, black and white children went to separate schools. In the mid-1900s, the laws began

hoping to find better jobs and a better life. So many African Americans left that the total **population** of the state fell. This happened at a time when most states were growing.

Today, about six out of ten people in the state are white. Almost four out of ten people are black.

to change. By 1986, all public schools in the state of Mississippi had to serve children of all races.

The Elizabeth Female Academy was the first college for women in the nation. It opened in the town of Washington in 1818. Alcorn State University was the first state college for African Americans. It was founded in 1871. Today, Mississippi State University is the largest university in the state. It is near Starkville.

Most people in this state are Christian. The Baptist faith is the most common religion. Methodists, Roman Catholics, and Jews also live in Mississippi.

Famous People of Mississippi

Richard Wright

Born: September 4, 1908, near Natchez, Mississippi

Died: November 28, 1960, Paris, France

Many great writers have come from this state. Richard Wright was one of the best. He grew up in a poor family and often faced harsh and unfair treatment from whites. After he grew up, he wrote books that showed how hard life was for black people. His first book, *Native Son*, became very famous. Wright moved to France in the late 1940s. He left the United States to **protest** the way black people were treated there.

The Land

Mississippi is a southern state that borders the Gulf of Mexico. It is not a large state, but it is a beautiful one. Lush forests cover more than one-half of the land. Lovely swamps, sandy beaches, and rivers also add to the state's charm. Magnolia trees grow all over Mississippi. The magnolia is both the state flower and the state tree.

The Delta

The Mississippi River is the second-longest river in the U.S. This huge river runs down the western edge of the state. Along the river is a flat, low area called the Delta. It was made by the river. For thousands of years, the river often overflowed its banks. Each time the waters fell back, they left behind rich black soil. This soil built up to form the Delta.

A riverboat carries tourists along the Mississippi River.

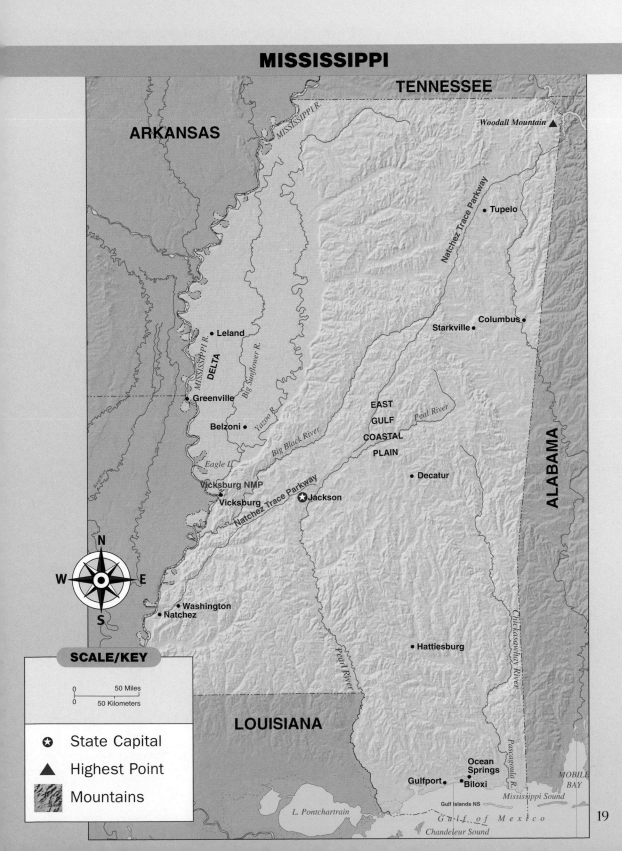

MISSISSIPPI

TENNESSEE

ARKANSAS

MISSISSIPPI R.

Woodall Mountain ▲

Natchez Trace Parkway

• Tupelo

• Leland

DELTA

MISSISSIPPI R.

Big Sunflower R.

Columbus •

Starkville •

• Greenville

Belzoni •

Yazoo

EAST
GULF
COASTAL
PLAIN

Peal River

Big Black River

Eagle L.

Vicksburg NMP

• Decatur

• Vicksburg

Natchez Trace Parkway

✪ Jackson

ALABAMA

N
W   E
S

• Washington
• Natchez

Chickasawhay River

• Hattiesburg

SCALE/KEY

0   50 Miles
0   50 Kilometers

Pearl River

Pascagoula R.

LOUISIANA

Ocean
Springs
Gulfport •   • Biloxi

MOBILE
BAY

Mississippi Sound

Gulf Islands NS

✪ State Capital

▲ Highest Point

▨ Mountains

L. Pontchartrain

Gulf of Mexico

Chandeleur Sound

19

In the north, the Delta reaches all the way to the Yazoo River. It is up to 65 miles (105 km) wide in some places. Further south, it is less than 1 mile (1.5 km) wide.

Much of the Delta was once covered with big swamps called **bayous**. In the 1800s, settlers drained the bayous so they could

Major Rivers

Mississippi River
2,357 miles (3,792 km)

Big Black River
330 miles (531 km)

Yazoo River
189 miles (304 km)

plant cotton. The Delta's moist, rich soil helped the cotton growers become very wealthy.

East Gulf Coastal Plain

East of the Delta, **bluffs** mark the start of the East Gulf Coastal Plain. It covers

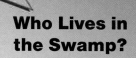

FUN FACTS

Who Lives in the Swamp?

Swamps can still be found in the Delta. Catfish, turtles, and alligators swim in the water. Snakes hunt nearby. Pelicans and long-legged birds, such as herons and egrets, make their homes here, too. Deer step quietly though the woods. Owls, hawks, mockingbirds, and woodpeckers perch in swamp oak, cypress, and cottonwood trees.

Swamps provide homes for all kinds of wildlife.

20

FUN FACTS

Wildlife Areas

Mississippi has set aside thirty-eight special wildlife areas. Thanks to these areas, the state has a huge number of white-tailed deer. The state is also known for its ducks and wild turkeys.

most of the rest of the state. Much of this region is made up of low hills. In some places, the hills are covered with pine, oak, and hickory trees. In others, prairie grasses once grew. Now, most of the prairie land is being used for farming.

The northeastern corner of the state has steep hills and deep, narrow valleys. These are the Tennessee River Hills. The highest point in the state is here. It is Woodall Mountain. At 806 feet (246 meters) high, it is one of the lowest high points in the United States.

In the south, palm and live oak trees grow. Sandy beaches line the Gulf of Mexico. Islands lie not far off shore in the warm waters of the Gulf.

The land near the shore is flat. When Hurricane Katrina hit, a huge wall of water surged over the low-lying shore and swept 6 miles (10 km) inland!

Climate

The state has a mild climate. Summers are long, humid, and hot. Winters are cool. The hills in the north are colder than the rest of the state. Rainfall is plentiful all over Mississippi, and snow sometimes falls in the north. Hurricanes are most likely in late summer and early fall.

Economy

For a very long time, farming was the main way of life here. Today, only about 2 percent of all workers have jobs on farms. Even so, farming is important. The leading farm products are chickens, beef cattle, cotton, and soybeans. Some farmers raise catfish. They raise these fish in ponds. Mississippi produces more farm-raised catfish than any other state.

The state's forests and the Gulf of Mexico also provide jobs. Loggers cut down trees to be made into lumber and paper. Fishermen net shrimp and herring.

On catfish farms, fish are raised in special pens in the water.

Making Goods and Providing Services

Factories bring money into the state. Some factories make food products. These products include frozen fish and sausage. Other factories make sofas and chairs, parts for cars, clothing, and even big ships. Jackson is the state's manufacturing center. The main shipping center is Gulfport.

Many workers help other people in their jobs. These workers are called service workers. Some of the state's service workers have jobs in schools or hospitals. Others work in hotels, restaurants, museums, theaters, or parks. Many service workers have jobs that help the thousands of tourists who visit this state each year.

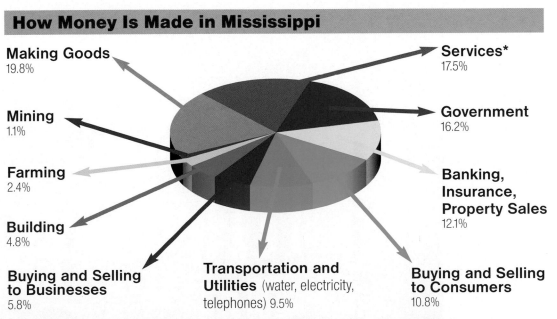

How Money Is Made in Mississippi

Making Goods
19.8%

Mining
1.1%

Farming
2.4%

Building
4.8%

Buying and Selling to Businesses
5.8%

Transportation and Utilities (water, electricity, telephones) 9.5%

Buying and Selling to Consumers
10.8%

Services*
17.5%

Government
16.2%

Banking, Insurance, Property Sales
12.1%

* Services include jobs in hotels, restaurants, auto repair, medicine, teaching, and entertainment.

Government

Jackson is Mississippi's capital city. This is where the state's leaders work. Mississippi's state government has three parts. They are the executive, legislative, and judicial branches.

Executive Branch

The governor leads the executive branch. This branch makes sure state laws are carried out. The lieutenant governor helps the governor. A group of people known as the **cabinet** also help.

The Mississippi state capitol was built on the site of an old prison.

Legislative Branch

The job of the legislative branch is to make state laws. The legislature is made up of two groups. These groups are the Senate and the House of Representatives. These two groups work together.

Judicial Branch

Judges and courts make up the judicial branch. Judges and courts may decide whether people who have

The Governor's Mansion was built in 1842. It is the second oldest governor's mansion in the United States.

been **accused of** committing crimes are guilty.

Local Governments

The state of Mississippi has eighty-two counties. Each county is led by a group of five people. Within the counties, some cities and towns are led by a mayor.

MISSISSIPPI'S STATE GOVERNMENT

Executive		Legislative		Judicial	
Office	**Length of Term**	**Body**	**Length of Term**	**Court**	**Length of Term**
Governor	4 years	Senate (52 members)	4 years	Supreme (9 justices)	8 years
Lieutenant Governor	4 years	House of Representatives (122 members)	4 years	Court of Appeals (10 judges)	8 years

Things to See and Do

Mississippi has lovely state parks and national forests. They offer great hiking and horseback riding trails. You can canoe and fish in the rivers or sleep in a tent in the forest.

The Natchez Trace is an old trail that winds across the state. Long ago, Natives and settlers traveled on this path. Today, a parkway follows the route. Hikers still walk parts of this beautiful trail.

The sandy beaches of the Gulf Coast are great vacation spots. In 2005, Hurricane Katrina damaged the coast.

The Natchez Trace Trail is a great place to go bird watching, horseback riding, and hiking.

The state is working hard to restore this area.

History Comes Alive

Learning about history is fun in Mississippi. Many towns have Civil War battlefields. Vicksburg has one of the best. At this site, you can see old cannons, rebuilt trenches, and a real gunboat.

In Natchez, you can visit stately old **mansions**, where rich plantation owners once lived. You can visit Fort Rosalie, too. It was one of the first European forts in the region. The Grand Village of the Natchez Indians is in Natchez, too. It has a museum and a Native house. In the month of March, a real **powwow** is held there. You can enjoy Native food, music, dancing, and crafts.

FUN FACTS

Catfish, Anyone?

The town of Belzoni is the Catfish Capital of the World. Once each year, the World Catfish Festival takes place there. You can join a catfish-eating contest and see the Catfish Queen crowned. You can enjoy a fish fry, too — the world's largest, of course!

Natchez is home to many lovely old mansions. This one is called Auburn. It is open for tours.

Famous People of Mississippi

Elvis Presley

Born: January 8, 1935, Tupelo, Mississippi

Died: August 16, 1977, Memphis, Tennessee

Elvis Presley got his first guitar when he was eleven years old. Just seven years later, he made his first record. It was a present for his mother. His records were soon being played by radio stations all around the country. Over the years, he had thirty number one hits, including "Don't Be Cruel" and "Heartbreak Hotel." He is still remembered as "The King of Rock 'n' Roll."

Museums and Music

Jackson is home to a great natural science museum. It has all kinds of alligators, fish, turtles, and other creatures. The city also has a sports museum and hall of fame. Its hands-on exhibits are fun for all.

Mississippi is famous for a kind of music known as Delta blues. This kind of music was created by African Americans who lived in the Delta area. Each year in June, Leland hosts the Highway 61 Blues Festival.

This festival attracts blues lovers from far and wide.

Sports

This state is known for its college sports. Football, baseball, and basketball games attract many fans. The hottest sports event of the year is a football game. Mississippi State faces its **rival**, the University of Mississippi. The stands are packed with loyal fans who cheer for their teams.

The University of Florida Gators go up for an incomplete pass against the Mississippi State Bulldogs.

Famous People of Mississippi

Jim Henson

Born: September 24, 1936, Greenville, Mississippi

Died: May 16, 1990, New York, New York

When Jim Henson was a child, he loved to draw and paint. He worked with puppets on a local TV show as a teenager. He soon created his own puppet show, *Sam and his Friends*. Henson called his puppets Muppets. Kermit the Frog, Big Bird, and other Muppets first appeared on *Sesame Street* in 1969. After that, Henson made TV shows of his own. He also made six Muppet movies.

accused of — blamed for

bayous — marshy areas with slow-moving water

bluffs — steep cliffs or banks

cabinet — a team of people who help a leader

colony — a group of people living in a new land but being controlled by the place they came from

factories — buildings where products are made

mansions — very large houses with many rooms

plantations — very large farms, usually in a warm climate, that grow cotton, tea, or other big crops

population — the number of people in a place, such as a city, town, or state

powwow — a Native American gathering

protest — to speak out against something

reservation — land set aside by the government for a certain purpose

riot — wild, violent behavior by an angry crowd

rival — one of two people or teams that are trying to win a game or contest

secede — to break away

segregated — separated by race

territory — an area that belongs to a country

tourists — people who travel for fun

Union — the United States of America

Books

Everywhere in Mississippi. Laurie Parker (Quail Ridge Press)

How Thunder and Lightning Came to Be: A Choctaw Legend. Beatrice Orcutt Harrell (Dial)

Life on a Southern Plantation. Picture the Past (series). Sally Senzell Isaacs (Heinemann)

Mississippi. From Sea to Shining Sea (series). Barbara A. Somervill (Children's Press)

The Mississippi River. Rivers of North America (series). Jen Green (Gareth Stevens)

My First Book About Mississippi. Carole Marsh (Gallopade International)

Web Sites

Classbrain.com: State Reports
classbrain.com/artstate/publish/cat_index_31.shtml

Enchanted Learning
www.enchantedlearning.com/usa/states/mississippi

Mississippi Resources
www.visitmississippi.org/resources

Official Mississippi Web Site
www.mississippi.gov/index.jsp

INDEX

★ ★